500

GEOGRAPHY FACTS
FASCINATING FACTS FOR GEOGRAPHERS YOUNG & OLD

COUNTRIES

Afghanistan is known for its beautiful blue gemstone, lapis lazuli, which has been mined there for over 6,000 years.

Albania is home to the largest amphitheater in the Balkans, the Amphitheatre of Durres, which can seat up to 20,000 people.

Algeria is the largest country in Africa and the 10th largest country in the world. It covers an area of approximately 2.38 million square kilometers.

Andorra is one of the smallest countries in Europe, with a population of just over 77,000 people.

Angola is known for having one of the highest numbers of natural resources in Africa, including diamonds and oil.

Antigua and Barbuda is made up of two islands and has a population of just over 100,000 people.

Argentina is the eighth largest country in the world and is known for being the birthplace of the tango dance.

Armenia is home to the world's oldest winery, with evidence of wine production dating back to 4,000 BC.

Australia is the world's largest island and smallest continent, and is home to many unique animals such as kangaroos and koalas.

Bahrain is a small island nation in the Persian Gulf, and is home to the world's largest underwater theme park.

Bangladesh is the world's eighth most populous country, and is known for its production of high-quality textiles and garments.

Barbados is known for being the birthplace of the pop singer Rihanna, as well as for its beautiful beaches and coral reefs.

Belarus is sometimes called the "last dictatorship in Europe," due to the country's authoritarian government.

Belgium is known for its delicious chocolate, waffles, and beer, as well as for being the headquarters of the European Union.

Belize is home to the second largest coral reef system in the world, the Belize Barrier Reef.

Benin is known for its unique voodoo culture, which includes traditional rituals and dances.

Bhutan is a small Himalayan kingdom that measures its success by Gross National Happiness, rather than Gross Domestic Product.

Bolivia is known for its diverse landscape, which includes the Andes mountains, the Amazon rainforest, and the high-altitude Lake Titicaca.

Bosnia and Herzegovina is known for its stunning natural beauty, including the Kravice Waterfalls, which are over 25 meters high and located in the southern part of the country.

Botswana has the world's largest population of African elephants, with more than 135,000 living in the country's protected areas.

Brazil is home to the Amazon Rainforest, which is the largest rainforest in the world and covers about 40% of South America.

Brunei is one of the world's smallest countries and is located on the island of Borneo in Southeast Asia.

Bulgaria is home to the oldest continuously inhabited city in Europe, Plovdiv, which was founded around 6,000 years ago.

Burkina Faso is a landlocked country in West Africa and its name translates to "land of the honest men".

Another fun fact is that Burkina Faso is home to a very special type of tree called the baobab. These trees can live for thousands of years, and they can grow to be over 80 feet tall!

Burundi is one of the smallest countries in Africa and is known as the "heart of Africa" due to its location in the center of the continent.

Cabo Verde is a great place to see sea turtles! There are several different types of sea turtles that live in the waters around the islands, and during nesting season (which is usually from July to October), you can watch baby turtles hatch and make their way to the ocean.

Cambodia is home to the largest religious monument in the world, Angkor Wat, which attracts millions of visitors each year.

Cameroon is the only country in the world that has a star-shaped flag.

Canada is the second largest country in the world, and is home to the longest coastline of any country.

Cape Verde is an archipelago of 10 volcanic islands off the coast of West Africa, and is known for its beautiful beaches and diverse marine life.

Central African Republic is home to some of the last remaining forest elephants in Africa, as well as to rare species like the bongo antelope and the giant eland.

The Central African Republic is known for its rainforests and wildlife, including forest elephants and gorillas.

Chad is home to Lake Chad, which is the largest wetland in the Sahel region of Africa, and supports over 10 million people.

Chile is the longest country in the world, stretching over 4,300 km from north to south.

China is the most populous country in the world, and is home to some of the world's most iconic landmarks like the Great Wall of China and the Forbidden City.

Colombia is known for producing some of the world's best coffee, and is also home to the world's largest butterfly sanctuary.

Comoros is an archipelago of four volcanic islands in the Indian Ocean, and is known for its unique blend of African, Arabic, and French cultures.

The Congo Basin rainforest in Congo is the second-largest rainforest in the world, after the Amazon.

Costa Rica is home to over 500,000 species of animals and plants, making up over 5% of the world's biodiversity.

Côte d'Ivoire is a country in West Africa and is the world's largest exporter of cocoa beans, which are used to make chocolate.

The Plitvice Lakes National Park in Croatia is a UNESCO World Heritage site known for its beautiful waterfalls and turquoise lakes.

Cuba is famous for its classic cars from the 1950s, which are still used as taxis and tourist attractions today.

The Mediterranean island of Cyprus is home to the oldest wine label in the world, Commandaria, which dates back to 800 BC.

The Czech Republic is known for its beautiful castles, including the famous Prague Castle, which is the largest ancient castle in the world.

The Congo River, which runs through the Democratic Republic of the Congo, is the deepest river in the world, with a depth of over 220 meters (720 feet).

Denmark is known for its strong cycling culture, with over 12,000 km of bike paths and dedicated bike lanes in its cities.

Djibouti is home to the lowest point in Africa, Lake Assal, which sits 155 meters below sea level.

Dominica is known as the "Nature Island" of the Caribbean, and is home to lush rainforests, waterfalls, and hot springs.

The Dominican Republic is home to the Pico Duarte, the highest peak in the Caribbean, standing at 3,098 meters (10,164 feet).

Ecuador is home to the Galapagos Islands, which are known for their unique wildlife and inspired Charles Darwin's theory of evolution.

Egypt is home to some of the world's most iconic landmarks like the Pyramids of Giza and the Sphinx.

El Salvador is the smallest country in Central America, but it's home to over 20 active volcanoes and has a rich history and culture.

Located on the equator, this small country is home to one of Africa's largest oil reserves.

Eritrea is home to the world's largest deposit of salt, located in the Danakil Depression.

Estonia is known for its digital innovations, with over 99% of public services available online.

Eswatini is known for its traditional culture, including the famous Umhlanga Reed Dance, where thousands of young women dance in honor of the Queen Mother.

Ethiopia is home to one of the oldest continuous Christian civilizations in the world, with Christianity dating back to the 4th century AD.

Fiji is an archipelago of over 300 islands in the South Pacific, and is known for its stunning beaches, coral reefs, and crystal-clear waters.

Finland is known as the "Land of a Thousand Lakes," and is home to over 188,000 lakes.

France is the most visited country in the world, with over 89 million visitors in 2019, and is known for its rich history, culture, and cuisine.

Gabon is one of the most forested countries in Africa, with over 85% of its land covered by tropical rainforest.

Gambia is one of the smallest countries in Africa, but it's home to over 500 species of birds, making it a popular destination for birdwatching.

Georgia is known for its wine culture, with over 500 indigenous grape varieties and the world's first cultivated grapevines, dating back over 8,000 years.

Germany is the largest country in Europe, and is known for its engineering and technological innovations, including the automobile and the printing press.

The name Ghana means "warrior king" in the Soninke language, and the country is known for its rich history of powerful empires and kingdoms.

Greece is known for its ancient civilization and mythology, including famous figures like Alexander the Great and the gods and goddesses of Olympus.

Haiti is home to the Citadelle Laferrière, the largest fortress in the Americas, which was built in the early 19th century.

Honduras is home to the ancient Mayan city of Copán, which is a UNESCO World Heritage site and contains some of the most impressive Mayan ruins in Central America.

Hungary is known for its thermal baths, with over 1,000 hot springs across the country and dozens of public baths in Budapest alone.

Iceland is known as the "Land of Fire and Ice," with active volcanoes, glaciers, and geysers dotting the landscape.

India is the world's largest democracy, and is known for its diverse culture, cuisine, and history, including the Taj Mahal, one of the world's most iconic landmarks.

Indonesia is the world's largest archipelago, consisting of over 17,000 islands, and is home to some of the most biodiverse habitats on earth, including the Komodo dragon and the orangutan.

Italy is home to the oldest university in Europe, the University of Bologna, which was founded in 1088.

Jamaica is known for its music, including reggae and ska, and is the birthplace of many famous musicians, including Bob Marley.

Japan is known for its technological innovations, including robotics and bullet trains, as well as its rich culture and history, including samurai warriors and geisha.

Jordan is home to Petra, an ancient city carved into sandstone cliffs that is one of the New Seven .

Kazakhstan is the world's ninth-largest country by land area and is also the largest landlocked country in the world.

Kenya is home to some of the world's most famous wildlife reserves, including the Maasai Mara and Amboseli National Park.

Kiribati is the only country in the world that is situated in all four hemispheres.

Kuwait is one of the world's leading oil producers, and oil exports account for over half of its GDP.

Kyrgyzstan is home to the largest natural lake in Central Asia, Issyk-Kul, which is also one of the world's largest high-altitude lakes.

Laos is home to the famous Mekong River, which is one of the longest rivers in the world.

Latvia is known for its dense forests, which cover more than half of the country.

Lebanon is home to the oldest continuously inhabited city in the world, Byblos, which dates back over 7,000 years.

Lesotho is one of only three countries in the world that is completely surrounded by another country (South Africa).

Liberia was founded by freed American slaves in 1822 and was the first African country to gain independence from a European colonial power (in this case, the United States).

Libya is home to the ancient Roman city of Leptis Magna, which is one of the best-preserved Roman cities in the world.

Liechtenstein is one of the smallest countries in the world and is also one of only two doubly landlocked countries (meaning it is landlocked by countries that are also landlocked).

Madagascar is home to some of the most unique and diverse wildlife in the world, including lemurs, chameleons, and more.

Malawi is known as the "Warm Heart of Africa" because of its friendly people and welcoming culture.

Malaysia is known for its stunning beaches, tropical rainforests, and diverse cultural heritage.

Mali is home to the ancient city of Timbuktu, which was once a thriving center of Islamic scholarship and trade.

Malta is one of the smallest and most densely populated countries in the world, with a population of just over 500,000 people.

The ancient city of Teotihuacan, located near Mexico City, is home to some of the largest and most impressive pyramids in the world.

Namibia is home to the world's largest sand dunes, which can reach heights of up to 300 meters (1,000 feet).

Nauru is the smallest island nation in the world, with a total land area of just 21 square kilometers (8 square miles).

Nepal is home to eight of the ten highest mountains in the world, including Mount Everest, the tallest mountain in the world.

New Zealand is home to some of the world's most stunning natural landscapes, including glaciers, fiords, and volcanoes.

Nicaragua is home to Lake Nicaragua, the largest lake in Central America and one of the few freshwater lakes in the world that

Pakistan is home to the world's second-highest mountain peak, K2, which stands at 28,251 feet (8,611 meters).

The national symbol of Portugal is the Rooster: The Barcelos Rooster is a colorful and iconic emblem of Portugal that represents honesty, integrity, and good luck.

Qatar is the richest country in the world per capita, thanks to its vast oil and natural gas reserves.

Romania is home to Europe's largest population of brown bears, with around 6,000 of these majestic animals living in the country's vast forests.

Russia is the largest country in the world, covering over 17 million square kilometers of land.

Rwanda is known as the "Land of a Thousand Hills" due to its beautiful, hilly terrain.

Saint Kitts and Nevis is the smallest sovereign state in the Americas, both in terms of land area and population.

Saint Lucia is known for its stunning natural beauty, including the towering Pitons, two volcanic spires that rise out of the Caribbean Sea.

San Marino is the oldest surviving sovereign state in the world, having been founded in the year 301 AD.

Saudi Arabia is home to the world's largest oil reserves, which have helped fuel the country's rapid economic growth over the past several decades.

Senegal is home to one of the largest and most vibrant markets in West Africa, the Sandaga Market in the capital city of Dakar.

Serbia is known for its rich cultural heritage, including the historic city of Belgrade, which has been inhabited for over 7,000 years.

Sierra Leone is home to the world's largest diamond ever discovered, the 969-carat Star of Sierra Leone, which was found in 1972.

Singapore is one of the most densely populated countries in the world, with over 5.5 million people living on an island just 719 square kilometers in size.

Singapore is the world's only island city-state, meaning it is a sovereign city that is also considered a country.

Slovakia is home to the largest castle complex in the world, the Spiš Castle.

Slovakia is known for its stunning natural beauty, including the Tatra Mountains, a range of peaks that straddle the border with Poland.

Slovenia is home to the world's largest underground canyon, the Skocjan Caves, which feature an underground river and an enormous chamber known as the "Hall of Giants."

Slovenia is the only country in Europe that combines the Alps, the Mediterranean, the Pannonian Plain, and the Karst in one region.

The Solomon Islands are an archipelago of 900 islands in the South Pacific, known for their beautiful coral reefs and vibrant marine life.

Somalia is believed to be the birthplace of the human species, with important fossil finds such as the 3.2 million-year-old Lucy.

Somalia is home to one of the world's longest coastlines, stretching over 3,300 kilometers along the Indian Ocean and the Gulf of Aden.

South Africa is home to some of the world's most iconic wildlife, including lions, elephants, rhinos, and leopards, which can be seen on safari in the country's many national parks and game reserves.

South Africa is the only country in the world to have three capitals: Pretoria (executive), Bloemfontein (judicial), and Cape Town (legislative).

South Sudan is the world's youngest country, having gained independence from Sudan in 2011 after decades of civil war.

Spain has the second-highest number of UNESCO World Heritage sites in the world, with 48 sites.

Thailand is known as the "Land of Smiles" due to the friendliness of its people.

The Bahamas is an archipelago made up of more than 700 islands, and is known for its beautiful beaches and crystal-clear waters.

The Maldives is the lowest-lying country in the world, with an average elevation of just 1.5 meters (5 feet) above sea level.

The Netherlands is known for its beautiful tulip fields and windmills, as well as its vibrant cities like Amsterdam and Rotterdam.

The Seychelles is an made up of a series of 115 islands in the Indian Ocean, known for its pristine beaches, crystal-clear waters, and diverse marine life.

Timor-Leste is one of the world's youngest countries, gaining independence in 2002.

Togo is the world's fourth-largest producer of phosphate, a mineral used to make fertilizer and other products.

Tonga is the only country in the South Pacific that has never been colonized by a foreign power.

Turkey is the only country that is both in Europe and Asia, with a portion of its territory in each continent.

Uganda is the world's second-largest producer of bananas after India.

Ukraine is the largest country entirely within Europe, with an area of 603,628 square kilometers.

United Arab Emirates is home to the tallest building in the world, the Burj Khalifa, which stands at 828 meters tall.

United Kingdom is the birthplace of many famous bands and musicians, including The Beatles, Rolling Stones, and Adele.

United States of America is the third-largest country in the world, both by area and by population.

Vatican City is the smallest country in the world, with an area of only 0.44 square kilometers.

Venezuela has the world's highest uninterrupted waterfall, Angel Falls, which stands at 979 meters tall.

Vietnam is the world's second-largest coffee producer after Brazil.

Wales is part of the United Kingdom, but it has its own distinct culture and language, which is spoken by about 20% of the population.

Western Sahara is a disputed territory between Morocco and the Polisario Front, which seeks independence for the area.

Yemen is one of the oldest centers of civilization in the world, with a rich cultural and historical heritage dating back over 3,000 years. It was once known as "Arabia Felix" or "Happy Arabia" due to its fertile lands and bountiful resources.

Yemen is the ancestral homeland of the Queen of Sheba, a legendary queen who ruled over a vast kingdom in ancient times.

Zambia is home to one of the largest waterfalls in the world, Victoria Falls, which is also known as Mosi-oa-Tunya or "The Smoke that Thunders".

Zambia is home to Victoria Falls, one of the largest and most spectacular waterfalls in the world. It is located on the Zambezi River and is over 1.7 km wide and 108 meters tall. It is considered one of the Seven Natural .

Zimbabwe is home to the ancient ruins of Great Zimbabwe, which was once the capital of the Kingdom of Zimbabwe in the 11th century. The ruins consist of massive stone walls and towers that were built without mortar and are considered one of the most impressive ancient structures in Africa.

Capital Cities

London (United Kingdom) – It is home to the world-famous Big Ben clock tower, which weighs over 13 tons and stands at over 96 meters tall.

Paris (France) – It is known as the "City of Light" because it was one of the first cities to have street lighting, starting in the 17th century.

Madrid (Spain) – It is the highest capital city in Europe, located at an altitude of over 650 meters above sea level.

Lisbon (Portugal) – It is the oldest city in Western Europe, founded by the Phoenicians in 1200 BC.

Dublin (Ireland) – It is home to the famous Guinness Storehouse, a seven-story museum dedicated to the history and production of Guinness beer.

Rome (Italy) – It is known as the "Eternal City" because of its ancient history, which dates back over 2,500 years.

Berlin (Germany) – It has the largest zoo in Europe, the Berlin Zoo, which is home to over 19,000 animals from around the world.

Athens (Greece) – It is the birthplace of democracy and the site of the famous Acropolis, a hilltop citadel that contains several ancient temples and monuments.

Vienna (Austria) – It is known for its coffee culture, with many historic coffee houses that date back to the 19th century.

Brussels (Belgium) – It is the capital of the European Union and the headquarters of NATO, the North Atlantic Treaty Organization.

Copenhagen (Denmark) - It is home to the famous Little Mermaid statue, inspired by the fairy tale by Hans Christian Andersen.

Stockholm (Sweden) - It is built on 14 islands and is surrounded by waterways, making it a popular destination for boat tours and cruises.

Oslo (Norway) - It is the fastest-growing capital city in Europe, with a population that has more than doubled since 1960.

Helsinki (Finland) - It is known for its unique architecture, including the famous Temppeliaukio Church, which is carved into a solid rock formation.

Reykjavik (Iceland) - It is the northernmost capital city in the world and is known for its natural hot springs and geothermal pools.

Moscow (Russia) – It is home to the famous Red Square, a historic plaza that has been the site of many important events in Russian history.

Amsterdam (Netherlands) – It is known for its canals and narrow streets, and is home to many famous museums, including the Van Gogh Museum and the Rijksmuseum.

Bern (Switzerland) – It is the capital of Switzerland and is known for its picturesque old town, which is a UNESCO World Heritage site.

Warsaw (Poland) – It has a rich cultural heritage and is known for its historic Old Town, which was rebuilt after being destroyed during World War II.

Prague (Czech Republic) – It is known for its beautiful architecture, including the famous Charles Bridge, which dates back to the 14th century.

Lima (Peru) - It has a unique weather pattern called "la garúa," a persistent mist that occurs during the winter months.

Tegucigalpa (Honduras) - It is the only capital city in Central America that doesn't have a cathedral.

San Salvador (El Salvador) - It is the smallest and most densely populated capital city in Central America.

San José (Costa Rica) - It has a vibrant arts and culture scene, with many museums, galleries, and theaters throughout the city.

Panama City (Panama) - It is home to the Panama Canal, an engineering marvel that connects the Atlantic and Pacific oceans.

Havana (Cuba) - It is known for its colorful vintage cars, which are a major tourist attraction and an iconic symbol of the city.

Santo Domingo (Dominican Republic) - It is the oldest continuously inhabited city in the New World, founded by Christopher Columbus's brother in 1496.

Port-au-Prince (Haiti) - It is home to the Iron Market, a bustling marketplace that sells everything from fresh produce to voodoo charms.

Nassau (Bahamas) - It is located on the island of New Providence and is known for its beautiful beaches and crystal-clear waters.

Kingston (Jamaica) - It is the birthplace of reggae music and the home of the Bob Marley Museum, dedicated to the famous musician and his legacy.

Castries (Saint Lucia) - It is surrounded by beautiful beaches and lush rainforests, making it a popular destination for tourists.

Bridgetown (Barbados) - It is known for its rum distilleries and is home to the famous Mount Gay Rum brand.

Roseau (Dominica) - It is located on the island of Dominica, known as the "Nature Island" for its abundant rainforests, waterfalls, and hot springs.

Saint John's (Antigua and Barbuda) - It is located on the island of Antigua and is known for its beautiful beaches and historic architecture.

Georgetown (Guyana) - It is home to the world's tallest wooden building, St. George's Cathedral, which was built in the late 19th century.

Paramaribo (Suriname) – It is located on the Suriname River and is known for its multicultural population and diverse cuisine.

Port of Spain (Trinidad and Tobago) – It is home to the famous Carnival celebration, a colorful festival of music, dance, and costumes that takes place every February.

Belmopan (Belize) – It is the smallest capital city in Central America, with a population of just over 20,000.

Budapest (Hungary) – It is the only capital city in the world that has thermal springs, and is known for its historic thermal baths and spas.

Bucharest (Romania) – It is home to the largest administrative building in the world, the Palace of the Parliament, which covers an area of over 330,000 square meters.

Belgrade (Serbia) – It is the only European capital city that lies at the confluence of two major rivers, the Danube and the Sava.

Zagreb (Croatia) – It is home to the Museum of Broken Relationships, which features objects and stories from failed relationships around the world.

Bratislava (Slovakia) – It is the only capital city that borders two independent countries, Austria and Hungary.

Ljubljana (Slovenia) – It is known for its beautiful bridges, including the Triple Bridge, which is a symbol of the city.

Vilnius (Lithuania) – It has one of the largest Old Towns in Europe, and is home to many historic buildings and monuments.

Riga (Latvia) - It has the largest collection of Art Nouveau buildings in the world, and is known for its beautiful architecture.

Tallinn (Estonia) - It has one of the best-preserved medieval Old Towns in Europe, and is a UNESCO World Heritage site.

Valletta (Malta) - It is the smallest capital city in the European Union, with a population of just over 6,000 people.

Nicosia (Cyprus) - It is the last divided capital city in the world, with a United Nations buffer zone separating the Greek and Turkish sides of the city.

Reykjavik (Iceland) - It is the world's northernmost capital city, and is known for its stunning natural beauty and outdoor activities.

Bern (Switzerland) – It is the capital of Switzerland and is known for its picturesque old town, which is a UNESCO World Heritage site.

Tbilisi (Georgia) – It is located at the crossroads of Europe and Asia, and is known for its unique architecture and cultural heritage.

Minsk (Belarus) – It is the capital of Belarus and is known for its wide streets, green parks, and Stalinist architecture.

Vaduz (Liechtenstein) – It is the capital of the tiny country of Liechtenstein, and is known for its beautiful castle and scenic mountain views.

Andorra la Vella (Andorra) – It is the highest capital city in Europe, located at an altitude of over 1,000 meters above sea level.

Monaco (Monaco) – It is the second-smallest country in the world, and is known for its luxurious casinos, yachts, and hotels.

San Marino (San Marino) – It is the oldest republic in the world, and is known for its beautiful medieval architecture and stunning mountain views.

Vatican City (Vatican City) – It is the smallest country in the world, and is home to many famous landmarks, including St. Peter's Basilica and the Sistine Chapel.

Beijing (China) – It has the largest public square in the world, Tiananmen Square, which covers an area of over 100 acres.

Tokyo (Japan) – It has more Michelin-starred restaurants than any other city in the world, and is known for its delicious cuisine.

Seoul (South Korea) - It has one of the largest underground shopping centers in the world, with over 5 miles of shops and restaurants.

New Delhi (India) - It has the world's largest spice market, Khari Baoli, which has been in operation for over 400 years.

Bangkok (Thailand) - It has the longest name of any city in the world, Krung Thep Mahanakhon Amon Rattanakosin Mahinthara Ayuthaya Mahadilok Phop Noppharat Ratchathani Burirom Udomratchaniwet Mahasathan Amon Piman Awatan Sathit Sakkathattiya Witsanukam Prasit.

Jakarta (Indonesia) - It is the largest city in Southeast Asia, with a population of over 10 million people.

Tehran (Iran) - It is home to the Milad Tower, which is the sixth-tallest tower in the world, and offers panoramic views of the city.

Ankara (Turkey) - It is the second-largest city in Turkey, and is known for its ancient citadel, historic mosques, and modern architecture.

Kuala Lumpur (Malaysia) - It is home to the Petronas Twin Towers, which were the tallest buildings in the world from 1998 to 2004.

Manila (Philippines) - It is the most densely populated city in the world, with over 42,000 people per square kilometer.

Riyadh (Saudi Arabia) - It is the largest city in Saudi Arabia, and is known for its modern skyscrapers, luxury shopping malls, and ancient ruins.

Ulaanbaatar (Mongolia) - It is the coldest capital city in the world, with an average temperature of -1°C (30°F) in January.

Hanoi (Vietnam) – It is home to the Ho Chi Minh Mausoleum, which is the final resting place of the Vietnamese revolutionary leader.

Phnom Penh (Cambodia) – It is located at the intersection of three major rivers, the Mekong, Tonle Sap, and Bassac.

Doha (Qatar) – It is the fastest-growing city in the world, with a population that has more than tripled in the last 20 years.

Buenos Aires (Argentina) – It is known as the "Paris of South America" due to its European architecture and vibrant cultural scene.

Brasilia (Brazil) – It was built in just four years and was designed to look like an airplane from above.

Santiago (Chile) – It is located in a valley surrounded by the Andes mountains, which makes for breathtaking views.

Bogota (Colombia) – It has the largest network of bike paths in Latin America, with over 300 miles of dedicated lanes.

Quito (Ecuador) – It is located just 15 miles south of the equator, which means the city has a year-round temperate climate.

Georgetown (Guyana) – It is the only city in South America that speaks English as its official language.

Asuncion (Paraguay) – It is one of the oldest cities in South America, founded in 1537 by Spanish explorer Juan de Salazar y Espinoza.

Lima (Peru) - It is known as the "Gastronomical Capital of the Americas" due to its delicious cuisine and world-renowned chefs.

Paramaribo (Suriname) - It is home to the largest wooden structure in South America, the St. Peter and Paul Cathedral.

Montevideo (Uruguay) - It is one of the most LGBTQ-friendly cities in South America, with a vibrant gay community and annual pride parade.

Caracas (Venezuela) - It is located at the foot of the Avila mountain range, which offers stunning views of the city and the Caribbean Sea.

Cairo (Egypt) - It is home to the Great Sphinx and the pyramids of Giza, which are some of the oldest and most recognizable landmarks in the world.

Algiers (Algeria) – It is known as the "White City" due to its many whitewashed buildings and houses.

Luanda (Angola) – It is home to the largest bay in Africa, which is surrounded by beautiful beaches and a bustling port.

Yaounde (Cameroon) – It is one of the greenest cities in Africa, with many parks and gardens throughout the city.

Bangui (Central African Republic) – It is located on the Ubangi River, which is a major tributary of the Congo River.

N'Djamena (Chad) – It is one of the hottest cities in the world, with temperatures often reaching over 40°C (104°F) in the summer.

Kinshasa (Democratic Republic of the Congo) – It is the largest city in the country and is known for its vibrant music scene and lively nightlife.

Djibouti City (Djibouti) – It is located at the southern entrance to the Red Sea, which makes it an important strategic location for international trade.

Addis Ababa (Ethiopia) – It is the highest capital city in Africa, located at an altitude of over 7,000 feet above sea level.

Accra (Ghana) – It is known for its colorful markets and street food, including the popular dish of jollof rice.

Nairobi (Kenya) – It is home to the Nairobi National Park, which is the only national park in the world located within a major city.

Mbabane (Eswatini) – It is the smallest capital city in Africa, with a population of just over 80,000 people.

Rabat (Morocco) – It is known for its beautiful beaches, colorful markets, and historic architecture.

Lagos (Nigeria) – It is the largest city in Africa by population and is known for its vibrant music, film, and fashion industries.

Pretoria (South Africa) – It is home to the Union Buildings, which are the official seat of the South African government and a popular tourist attraction.

Monrovia (Liberia) – It is named after James Monroe, the fifth President of the United States, who helped to establish Liberia as a colony for freed slaves.

Population & Tourism

The world's population is estimated to be over 7.9 billion people as of 2021.

China is the most populous country in the world, with a population of over 1.4 billion people.

The smallest country in the world by population is Vatican City, with just over 800 residents.

It is estimated that the world's population will reach 9.7 billion by 2050.

The United States is the third-most populous country in the world, with over 330 million people.

India is the second-most populous country in the world, with a population of over 1.3 billion people.

Tokyo, Japan is the most populous city in the world, with a population of over 37 million people in its metropolitan area.

The country with the lowest population density in the world is Mongolia, with just over 2 people per square kilometer.

Nigeria is projected to become the world's third-most populous country by 2050, with a population of over 400 million people.

Monaco has the highest population density in the world, with over 19,000 people per square kilometer.

The country with the highest birth rate in the world is Niger, with an average of 7.2 births per woman.

The world's population has more than tripled in the past 100 years, from 2.5 billion in 1950 to over 7.9 billion in 2021.

The global population growth rate has been decreasing over time, with a current rate of around 1.05%.

China's "One Child Policy," which was in effect from 1979 to 2015, was designed to limit population growth by allowing each couple to have only one child.

The world's population is not evenly distributed, with some regions, such as Asia and Africa, having much higher population densities than others.

The world's population is also becoming increasingly urbanized, with more people living in cities than in rural areas.

Japan has the oldest population in the world, with over 28% of its citizens aged 65 or older.

The fertility rate in developed countries tends to be lower than in developing countries, with some countries, such as Japan and Italy, experiencing declining populations as a result.

The population of the world's largest cities is projected to continue to grow, with some estimates suggesting that by 2100, over 85% of the world's population will live in cities.

The United Nations predicts that by 2100, the world's population will reach its peak at around 11 billion people before gradually declining.

The current world population is estimated to be about 50 times larger than it was during the time of the ancient Egyptians.

Some countries, such as Singapore, have implemented policies to encourage population growth due to concerns about aging populations and declining birth rates.

The world's most populous country, China, has implemented a number of policies aimed at reducing population growth, including the "Two Child Policy" introduced in 2016.

The population of some countries, such as Germany, is projected to decline significantly over the next few decades due to low birth rates and an aging population.

Over 50% of the world's population lives in just 7 countries: China, India, the United States, Indonesia, Brazil, Pakistan, and Nigeria.

Tourism is one of the largest and fastest-growing industries in the world, generating trillions of dollars in revenue each year.

Airbnb, a popular online platform for booking accommodations, was founded in 2008 and has since become a major player in the tourism industry.

Ecotourism, which focuses on sustainable and responsible travel to natural areas, is becoming increasingly popular as people seek to minimize their impact on the environment.

In 2019, the United Nations declared that the year 2020 would be the International Year of Tourism and Rural Development, highlighting the importance of tourism in supporting rural communities.

Many countries offer free walking tours led by locals, providing a unique and affordable way to explore a new city and learn about its history and culture.

Some countries, like Bhutan, have implemented policies to limit the number of tourists in order to preserve their culture and environment.

The concept of the modern hotel originated in the United States in the mid-19th century, with the opening of the Tremont House in Boston in 1829.

The Eiffel Tower in Paris was originally built as a temporary structure for the 1889 World's Fair, but became a permanent landmark due to its popularity with tourists.

The Great Wall of China is the world's most popular tourist attraction, with over 10 million visitors each year.

The Louvre Museum in Paris is the most visited art museum in the world, with over 10 million visitors each year.

The world's population is also getting older. This is because people are living longer due to advances in medicine and technology. By the year 2050, it's estimated that there will be more people over the age of 65 than under the age of 5!

The tallest water slide in the world is located in Brazil and stands over 140 feet tall.

The world's first theme park was opened in Denmark in 1843, and is still in operation today.

The world's largest hotel is the First World Hotel in Malaysia, which has over 7,000 rooms.

The world's largest indoor water park is located in Germany, covering over 200,000 square meters.

The world's largest roller coaster is located in New Jersey, USA, and is over 456 feet tall.

The world's most expensive hotel room is located in Geneva, Switzerland, and costs over $75,000 per night.

The world's most visited city by international tourists is Bangkok, Thailand, followed by Paris, France and London, England.

According to the Times Square Alliance, approximately 50 million people visit Times Square each year. It's one of the most popular tourist destinations in the world, known for its bright lights, towering billboards, and bustling atmosphere.

With advances in technology, virtual and augmented reality are increasingly being used to enhance the tourism experience, allowing travelers to "visit" destinations from the comfort of their own homes.

In Amsterdam, there is a museum dedicated entirely to cheese! It's called the Cheese Museum and visitors can learn about the history of cheese-making and even sample some of the delicious cheeses from around the world.

The oldest hotel in the world is called the Nishiyama Onsen Keiunkan and is located in Japan. It was founded in the year 705 and has been in operation for over 1,300 years!

The most visited tourist attraction in the UK is the British Museum in London, with over 6 million visitors annually.

The world's tallest hotel is located in Dubai and is called the Gevora Hotel. It has 75 floors and is 1,168 feet tall!

One of the most visited tourist attractions in Nigeria is the Olumo Rock, located in Abeokuta. It is a large outcrop of granite rocks that served as a fortress for the Egba people in the 19th century. Today, it is a popular tourist destination, with visitors climbing the rock to enjoy the spectacular view of the city and learn about the history and culture of the Egba people.

Rivers & Oceans

The longest river in the world is the Nile, which flows through 11 countries in Africa and spans over 4,135 miles (6,650 kilometers).

The Amazon River in South America is the largest river in terms of volume of water and carries more water than any other river in the world.

The Mississippi River in the United States is the fourth-longest river in the world and the longest river in North America.

The Yangtze River in China is the third-longest river in the world and the longest river in Asia.

Rivers play an important role in the water cycle by transporting water from the land to the oceans.

The Congo River in Africa is the deepest river in the world, with depths reaching over 700 feet (220 meters) in some places.

Rivers are often used for transportation, with many major cities located along the banks of rivers.

The Mekong River in Southeast Asia is home to over 1,000 different species of fish, making it one of the most biodiverse rivers in the world.

Some of the world's most famous and important cities, such as London, Paris, and Rome, were founded along rivers.

The Colorado River in the United States has carved out the Grand Canyon over millions of years, creating one of the world's most spectacular natural wonders.

The Ganges River in India is considered one of the holiest rivers in the world and is an important site for Hindu pilgrimages.

The Rhine River in Europe is one of the most important rivers in the continent, flowing through 6 countries and serving as a major transport route for goods and people.

The Pacific Ocean is the largest ocean in the world, covering over 60 million square miles.

Some species of jellyfish can glow in the dark, creating a beautiful bioluminescent effect in the water.

Some whales can communicate with each other over distances of thousands of miles through low-frequency sounds that travel long distances in water.

The Arctic Ocean is the smallest and shallowest of the world's oceans, but is home to many unique species adapted to the extreme cold.

The Atlantic Ocean is home to the longest mountain range in the world, called the Mid-Atlantic Ridge.

The deepest part of the ocean is the Mariana Trench, located in the Pacific Ocean, which reaches a depth of over 36,000 feet.

The Great Barrier Reef, located in the Coral Sea off the coast of Australia, is the largest coral reef system in the world.

The Indian Ocean is home to many unique marine species, such as the dugong and the coelacanth.

The oceans are also an important source of energy, with many countries using ocean currents and waves to generate electricity.

The oceans are also home to many different kinds of whales, dolphins, and porpoises, which are some of the most intelligent and social animals on the planet.

The oceans are an important source of food for many people around the world, with seafood being a staple in many cultures.

The oceans are an important source of recreation and relaxation for many people, with activities like surfing, boating, and swimming being popular all over the world.

The oceans are home to many different kinds of sharks, including the great white, tiger, and hammerhead.

The oceans are responsible for producing over 50% of the world's oxygen through the process of photosynthesis by marine plants.

The oceans contain over 20 million tons of gold, but it is too diluted to be extracted.

The oceans contain over 95% of the Earth's total water supply, but only 5% of it has been explored by humans.

The oceans contain over 99% of the world's living space.

The oceans play a critical role in regulating the Earth's climate by absorbing and releasing heat and carbon dioxide.

The Southern Ocean, also known as the Antarctic Ocean, surrounds Antarctica and is home to many penguins and other cold-adapted animals.

The tides are caused by the gravitational pull of the moon and the sun on the Earth's oceans.

The world's longest coastline belongs to Canada, stretching over 202,080 km.

Coastal areas are home to many important ecosystems such as coral reefs, mangroves, and wetlands, which support a wide variety of plant and animal life.

The coastal region is an important source of food for people around the world, with many coastal communities relying on fishing and aquaculture.

Coastal areas are popular tourist destinations due to their scenic beauty, recreational activities such as swimming, surfing, and boating, and cultural attractions such as coastal towns and historic landmarks.

The coast is constantly changing due to natural processes such as erosion, sedimentation, and sea level rise, as well as human activities such as development and pollution.

Some of the world's largest cities, such as New York City, Tokyo, and Mumbai, are located on the coast and are important centers of trade, commerce, and industry.

Coastal areas are vulnerable to such as hurricanes, tsunamis, and storm surges, which can cause significant damage and loss of life.

Lakes can be found on every continent on Earth.

The world's largest lake is the Caspian Sea, which is actually a saltwater lake.

Lake Baikal in Russia is the world's deepest lake, reaching a depth of over 5,300 feet. It contains about 20% of the world's unfrozen freshwater.

The Great Lakes of North America (Lake Superior, Lake Michigan, Lake Huron, Lake Erie, and Lake Ontario) are the largest group of freshwater lakes in the world by total area.

The largest lake in Africa is Lake Victoria, which is also the world's second-largest freshwater lake by area.

Lake Maracaibo in Venezuela is home to a phenomenon called Catatumbo lightning, which can produce nearly constant lightning for up to 10 hours a night.

A canal is a man-made waterway that is constructed for navigation, irrigation, or water supply purposes.

The first canals were built over 5,000 years ago in Mesopotamia (modern-day Iraq) for irrigation purposes.

Canals were important for transportation and trade during the Industrial Revolution in the 18th and 19th centuries.

The world's largest canal network is in Canada, with over 24,000 miles of canals and waterways.

The longest canal in the world is the Grand Canal in China, which is over 1,100 miles long.

Mountains, Deserts & Rainforests

The tallest mountain in the world is Mount Everest, which is located in the Himalayas in Asia and is over 29,000 feet tall.

Mountains are formed when tectonic plates collide and push the earth's crust upward.

The Andes Mountains in South America are the longest mountain range in the world, stretching over 4,000 miles.

The Rocky Mountains in North America are known for their beautiful scenery and are a popular destination for outdoor activities like hiking and skiing.

Mount Kilimanjaro in Africa is the highest mountain in Africa and is actually a dormant volcano.

The Swiss Alps are known for their beautiful snow-capped peaks and are a popular destination for skiing and snowboarding.

The Appalachian Mountains in North America are some of the oldest mountains in the world, dating back over 480 million years.

The Matterhorn, located in the Swiss Alps, is one of the most famous and recognizable mountains in the world.

The Himalayas are home to some of the world's most beautiful and diverse wildlife, including snow leopards, pandas, and yaks.

Many famous rivers, such as the Nile, Amazon, and Mississippi, originate in mountain ranges.

Mountains can create their own weather, with temperatures and conditions changing rapidly as you ascend.

The Great Smoky Mountains in North America are known for their beautiful foggy landscapes, which inspired their name.

The Alps, which are located in Europe, are home to a variety of cultures and languages, including French, German, and Italian.

The Himalayas are not only home to some of the tallest mountains in the world, but also some of the tallest trees, such as the Himalayan pine.

The tallest mountain in the world is actually underwater? It's called Mauna Kea, and it's located in Hawaii. Although its summit only rises 4,205 meters above sea level, Mauna Kea extends more than 10,000 meters below the ocean's surface, making its total height from base to summit over 14,000 meters!

The Rocky Mountains are home to many different kinds of wildlife, including elk, bighorn sheep, and black bears.

The Atlas Mountains in North Africa are home to many unique plant and animal species that are adapted to the arid desert climate.

Some mountains, like the Swiss Matterhorn, are famous for their challenging and dangerous climbing routes that require advanced skills and equipment.

The Pyrenees Mountains, which separate France and Spain, are home to many different cultures and languages, including Catalan and Basque.

Some mountains, like the Blue Mountains in Australia, are known for their beautiful blue hue caused by the release of oils from eucalyptus trees.

The Great Dividing Range in Australia is one of the longest mountain ranges in the world, stretching over 2,300 miles along the eastern coast.

The Drakensberg Mountains in South Africa are home to many ancient rock paintings created by the San people thousands of years ago.

The Alps are a popular destination for paragliding and other extreme sports, with many scenic and challenging spots for adventure-seekers.

The Carpathian Mountains in Europe are home to many different kinds of wildlife, including wolves, lynx, and bears.

Many famous cities are located in or near mountains, such as Denver in the United States and Innsbruck in Austria.

Deforestation, primarily for agricultural purposes, is a major threat to rainforests and their inhabitants.

Many rainforest animals, such as sloths and tree kangaroos, are adapted to living in the trees and rarely come down to the forest floor.

Rainforests are home to more than half of the world's plant and animal species, even though they cover only 6% of the Earth's surface.

Rainforests are incredibly biodiverse, with some trees in the Amazon rainforest hosting more than 40 different species of ants.

Rainforests are known as the "lungs of the Earth" because they produce around 20% of the world's oxygen.

Rainforests contain many medicinal plants that have been used for centuries by indigenous peoples to treat a variety of ailments.

Rainforests have some of the highest rainfall amounts in the world, receiving over 100 inches of rain per year in some areas.

The Amazon rainforest is so large that it spans nine countries in South America, including Brazil, Peru, and Colombia.

The Amazon rainforest, located primarily in Brazil, is the largest rainforest in the world, covering over 2.7 million square miles.

The canopy, or the uppermost layer of trees in a rainforest, can be over 100 feet tall and is home to many species of birds, insects, and mammals.

The Congo rainforest in Africa is the second-largest rainforest in the world, covering over 1.5 million square miles.

The rainforest is home to many endangered species, including orangutans, jaguars, and tigers.

The sound of a rainforest is often referred to as a "symphony" due to the diverse array of animal and insect calls and songs.

The world's largest flower, the Rafflesia arnoldii, is found in the rainforests of Southeast Asia and can grow up to three feet in diameter.

Antarctica is considered the world's largest desert because it receives very little precipitation despite being covered in snow and ice.

The driest desert in the world is the Atacama Desert in Chile, which has gone over 50 years without any significant rainfall.

Deserts can be extremely hot during the day, with temperatures reaching up to 120 degrees Fahrenheit, but can also be very cold at night.

The word "desert" comes from the Latin word "desertum," which means "an abandoned place."

The Mojave Desert in the United States is home to the Joshua tree, which is actually a type of yucca plant.

The Sonoran Desert in the United States is home to the saguaro cactus, which can grow up to 50 feet tall and live for over 200 years.

Some desert plants, such as cacti, have thick, fleshy stems that can store water for long periods of time.

Many animals in the desert, such as camels and kangaroo rats, have adapted to the harsh environment by storing water in their bodies and being active during the cooler parts of the day.

The Arabian Desert in the Middle East is the location of the largest continuous sand desert in the world, called the Rub' al Khali.

The Namib Desert in Africa is home to the Welwitschia plant, which can live for over 1,000 years and has only two leaves that continuously grow throughout its life.

Despite being a harsh and unforgiving environment, many people have lived in the desert for thousands of years, such as the Bedouin people of the Arabian Desert.

Our Climate

Climate is the average weather pattern of a region over a long period of time, typically 30 years.

The Earth's climate has changed throughout history, with periods of both warming and cooling. However, the current rate of warming is unprecedented and largely attributed to human activity.

The hottest temperature ever recorded on Earth was 134 degrees Fahrenheit (56.7 degrees Celsius) in Furnace Creek Ranch, California, in 1913.

The coldest temperature ever recorded on Earth was -128.6 degrees Fahrenheit (-89.2 degrees Celsius) in Antarctica in 1983.

The climate is influenced by many factors, including the sun, the Earth's rotation, the oceans, and the atmosphere.

The Earth's climate is divided into different zones, including the tropics, temperate zones, and polar regions, each with its own unique weather patterns and characteristics.

Climate change is causing rising sea levels, more frequent and intense heatwaves, and changes in precipitation patterns, among other impacts.

The Earth's atmosphere is made up of several layers, including the troposphere, stratosphere, mesosphere, and thermosphere.

The study of past climates is called paleoclimatology, which involves analyzing things like tree rings, ice cores, and sediment layers to understand how the climate has changed over time.

The World Meteorological Organization (WMO) is the United Nations agency responsible for the study of the Earth's climate and weather patterns.

Climate can vary greatly within a single country or region, leading to diverse landscapes and ecosystems. For example, the United States spans a wide range of climates, from the arctic tundra of Alaska to the subtropical wetlands of Florida.

Scientists use data from tree rings, ice cores, and other sources to study past climate patterns and help predict future changes.

Planting trees and other vegetation can help absorb carbon dioxide from the atmosphere and reduce the effects of climate change.

Renewable energy sources such as solar, wind, and hydro power are important solutions to reducing greenhouse gas emissions and addressing climate change.

The United Nations holds an annual climate change conference, known as COP (Conference of the Parties), where countries come together to discuss and coordinate global efforts to address climate change.

The polar regions are particularly sensitive to climate change, with the Arctic warming at twice the rate of the rest of the planet.

Climate change is affecting wildlife and their habitats, causing some species to become endangered or even extinct.

The greenhouse effect is a natural process that keeps the Earth's surface warm enough to support life. However, human activities are causing an increase in the concentration of greenhouse gases, which is leading to an enhanced greenhouse effect and resulting in a rise in global temperatures.

The Earth's climate is affected by natural factors such as volcanic eruptions, changes in the sun's intensity, and the Earth's orbit.

The Earth's temperature has risen by 1.1 degrees Celsius since the pre-industrial era, and is projected to rise by another 1.5 degrees Celsius by 2040.

Natural Disasters & Extreme Weather

Earthquakes happen when two tectonic plates rub against each other and release energy.

Earthquakes can happen anywhere, but they are most common along the Pacific Ocean in an area called the "Ring of Fire."

The largest earthquake ever recorded happened in Chile in 1960 and had a magnitude of 9.5.

Seismologists use a device called a seismometer to measure earthquakes.

The point underground where an earthquake originates is called the epicenter.

Earthquakes can cause tsunamis, which are giant waves that can cause a lot of damage.

The Richter Scale is used to measure the strength of earthquakes.

Earthquakes can last anywhere from a few seconds to a few minutes.

Some animals can sense when an earthquake is about to happen and will behave strangely.

Earthquakes can cause buildings to collapse and roads to buckle.

Aftershocks can occur after the main earthquake and can sometimes be just as strong.

Earthquakes can trigger landslides and avalanches.

The first recorded earthquake was in China in 132 AD.

Earthquakes can cause fires if gas lines rupture and spark.

Some people practice earthquake drills to prepare for earthquakes.

Earthquakes can cause liquefaction, which is when the ground turns to liquid-like soil and can swallow buildings and cars.

The San Andreas Fault in California is a well-known fault that is responsible for many earthquakes in the state.

Earthquakes can create cracks in the ground called fissures.

Earthquakes can cause changes to the Earth's rotation and the length of a day.

The word "seismic" comes from the Greek word "seismos," which means shaking or earthquake.

Tsunamis are giant waves that are caused by undersea earthquakes or volcanic eruptions.

The word "tsunami" comes from a Japanese term that means "harbor wave."

Tsunamis can travel at speeds of up to 500 miles per hour (800 km/h).

The height of a tsunami wave can reach up to 100 feet (30 meters) or more.

Tsunamis are not just limited to the ocean; they can also occur in lakes, rivers, and even swimming pools!

Tsunamis can travel across entire oceans, and can even reach coastlines on the opposite side of the world from where they originated.

Tsunamis can cause widespread destruction, including flooding, landslides, and damage to buildings and infrastructure.

The biggest tsunami on record occurred in 1958 in Lituya Bay, Alaska, and reached a height of 1,720 feet (524 meters).

Tsunamis can be detected and measured using specialized equipment called tsunami warning systems.

Tsunamis can be extremely dangerous, and it's important to know what to do in the event of a tsunami warning or evacuation order.

A volcano is a mountain that has a hole or vent where molten rock, ash, and gas escape during an eruption.

Some volcanic eruptions are relatively quiet, with slow-moving lava flows, while others are explosive and violent, with ash clouds and pyroclastic flows that can travel at hundreds of miles per hour.

The ash from a volcanic eruption can cause problems for airplanes, as it can damage engines and reduce visibility.

The eruption of Mount Tambora in Indonesia in 1815 was one of the largest volcanic eruptions in history, and caused a "year without a summer" in many parts of the world.

The largest volcano in the world, Mauna Loa in Hawaii, is over 13,600 feet tall.

There are several types of volcanoes, including shield volcanoes, cinder cone volcanoes, and composite volcanoes.

Volcanic eruptions can cause earthquakes, landslides, and tsunamis.

Volcanic eruptions can create new land, as molten rock cools and hardens to form solid rock.

Volcanoes can be found on every continent, including Antarctica.

When a volcano erupts, it can shoot ash and gas up to 20 miles into the sky.

Tornadoes are rapidly rotating columns of air that can reach wind speeds of up to 300 miles per hour (480 kilometers per hour).

Tornadoes are usually formed from severe thunderstorms, and can be accompanied by lightning, heavy rain, and hail.

The United States experiences the most tornadoes of any country in the world, with an average of 1,200 tornadoes per year.

Tornadoes are typically classified on the Fujita scale, which ranges from F0 to F5 based on wind speed and damage caused.

The most destructive tornadoes, rated F5 on the Fujita scale, can completely destroy homes and buildings, and can cause loss of life.

The fastest recorded tornado was the Tri-State Tornado, which struck parts of Missouri, Illinois, and Indiana in 1925 and reached wind speeds of up to 318 miles per hour (512 kilometers per hour).

Tornadoes can be difficult to predict, but meteorologists use radar and other advanced technology to monitor weather conditions and issue tornado warnings when necessary.

Tornadoes can last for just a few seconds or for over an hour, and can travel long distances before dissipating.

Super Typhoon Haiyan, which hit the Philippines in 2013, was one of the strongest typhoons ever recorded, with wind speeds reaching up to 195 mph.

The word "typhoon" comes from the Chinese word "tai fung," which means "great wind."

Some typhoons have caused significant historical events, such as the Mongol invasion of Japan in 1281, which was thwarted by a typhoon.

Hurricanes are large storms that form over warm ocean water in the Atlantic Ocean, Caribbean Sea, Gulf of Mexico, and eastern Pacific Ocean.

Hurricanes are given names in order to make it easier to track them and communicate information about them. Hurricane Katrina, which struck New Orleans in 2005, was one of the most destructive hurricanes in U.S. history.

The world's largest hailstone ever recorded was in Vivian, South Dakota, in 2010 and it was 8 inches in diameter and weighed almost 2 pounds.

Hailstones can be different colors, including white, clear, and even black.

Lightning bolts can travel at speeds of up to 224,000 miles per hour!

Lightning strikes the earth about 100 times every second.

The temperature of a lightning bolt can reach up to 30,000 degrees Celsius, which is hotter than the surface of the sun.

Lightning can strike the same place more than once. The Empire State Building in New York City gets struck by lightning an average of 23 times per year!

Lightning strikes can occur up to 10 miles away from a thunderstorm and can be deadly.

Wonders of the World

The Grand Canyon in Arizona, USA, was carved out by the Colorado River over millions of years and is over 1.6 kilometers deep.

The Grand Canyon is over 270 miles long and up to 18 miles wide.

The Zhangjiajie National Forest Park in China is known for its towering sandstone pillars that inspired the scenery in the movie Avatar.

The Angel Falls in Venezuela is the highest waterfall in the world, with a height of 979 meters.

The Victoria Falls on the border of Zambia and Zimbabwe in Africa is the largest waterfall in the world by area, measuring 1,708 meters wide and 108 meters high.

The Iguazu Falls on the border of Argentina and Brazil is a series of over 275 waterfalls that span nearly 3 kilometers.

The Ha Long Bay in Vietnam is a scenic area of over 1,500 islands and islets that are home to diverse flora and fauna.

The Great Blue Hole in Belize is a massive underwater sinkhole that is over 300 meters wide and 124 meters deep.

The Marble Caves in Chile are a series of caves and tunnels carved out by the waters of Lake General Carrera, and are known for their unique blue and grey marble formations.

The Grand Prismatic Spring in Yellowstone National Park, USA, is the largest hot spring in the country and is known for its colorful bacteria mats.

The northern lights are a natural light display that occurs in the polar regions of the Earth.

The northern lights are caused by electrically charged particles from the sun colliding with particles in the Earth's atmosphere.

The northern lights appear in different colors, including green, pink, purple, blue, and red.

The northern lights are most commonly seen in countries such as Norway, Sweden, Finland, Iceland, and Canada.

The northern lights can be seen from space and are visible from the International Space Station.

The northern lights can form different shapes, including arcs, curtains, and rays.

The northern lights can be very bright and can light up the entire sky.

The northern lights are more common during times of high solar activity, which happens every 11 years.

The Inuit people of Canada and Greenland have many legends and stories about the northern lights.

The southern lights, also known as aurora australis, are the southern hemisphere equivalent of the northern lights.

Printed in Great Britain
by Amazon

49143322R00062